NEW YEATS PAPERS X

I think all true poetry was conceived on the Mount of Transfiguration and there is revelation in it and the mingling of heaven and earth.

George W. Russell (Æ),
Song and Its Fountains, 1932.

GEORGE MILLS HARPER

THE MINGLING OF HEAVEN AND EARTH:
YEATS'S THEORY OF THEATRE

THE DOLMEN PRESS

CONTENTS

The Mingling of Heaven and Earth *page* 9
Notes on the text 41

General Editor: Liam Miller

This paper is a development of a lecture delivered to the Yeats International Summer School at Sligo on 26 August 1965.

PR
5907
.H 32

© 1975 George Mills Harper
ISBN 0 85105 269 X

Printed and published in the Republic of Ireland at the Dolmen Press, North Richmond Industrial Estate, North Richmond Street, Dublin 1.
First published 1975.
Distributed in the United States of America and in Canada by Humanities Press Inc., 171 First Avenue, Atlantic Highlands, N.J. 07716.

*To the Graduate Students
of my Yeats seminars
at Florida State University*

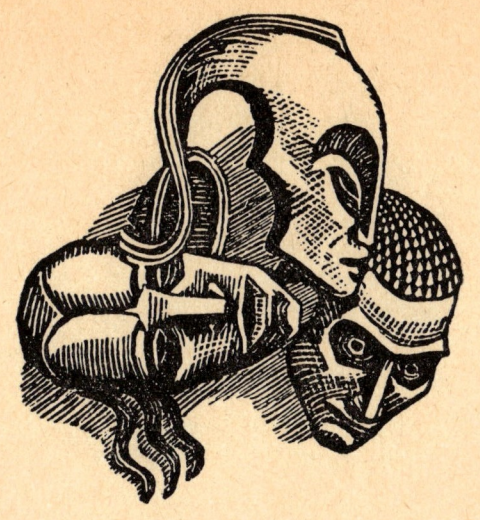

Masks: design based on masks made by Hildo Krop for *The Only Jealousy of Emer*, 1922, from the title page of *Wheels and Butterflies* by W. B. Yeats, 1934. Reproduced by kind permission of Macmillan, London and Basingstoke.

NOTE

Certain standard editions of Yeats's works frequently cited in the text are referred to by the following symbols, followed by page references:

- L: The Letters
- A: Autobiographies
- E: Explorations
- EI: Essays and Introductions

THE MINGLING OF HEAVEN AND EARTH

In light of the several books of recent years devoted to Yeats's drama,[1] I suppose that no serious critic would any longer agree with F. L. Lucas's rather contemptuous appraisal of Yeats's theatrical criticism as 'some rather thin dramatic theorizing' which 'he was tempted to' in order 'to justify his own practice.'[2] Nevertheless, despite the inordinate amount of time Yeats paid to the theatre for a period of several years, no full-length study of his theory of the theatre has yet been published, and perhaps will not be until additional unpublished materials are available — as, for example, the exchange of letters with Gordon Craig. This brief study makes no attempt at being definitive. It will, instead, bring together observations from the letters, essays, notes, and autobiographical writings to illustrate that Yeats had developed a coherent and comprehensive theory of the theatre.

We should not, I suppose, expect a systematic aesthetic from a man who insisted that 'intelligence has no organization whilst stupidity always has,'[3] and we must therefore be careful to avoid imposing a set of rules upon a gradually evolving theory which developed pragmatically as a result of day-to-day experience in the theatre and with the composition of drama.[4] It is equally clear, however, that Yeats, surveying his own experience and that of his friends and collaborators in the Irish dramatic movement, did indeed make a serious effort to analyze the aesthetic principles behind their creations, the reasons for their revolt against Victorian drama, and the validity of their accomplishment. Like Blake, Yeats was certain that he 'must Create a System or be enslav'd by another Man's.'[5] Although Yeats insisted in the first issue of *Samhain* (1901) that 'the arts are at their best when they are busy with battles that can never be won,' he had in fact started the periodical 'to defend the work' of the Irish dramatic movement, 'which is important because of the principles it is rooted in whatever be its fruits, and these principles are better told of in words that rose out of the need. . . .'[6] Because he was certain of the significance of his movement, Yeats felt it important to order and explain the critical principles which constitute the basis for his plays as well as those of

Lady Gregory, J. M. Synge, and others who wrote for the Abbey. The result is one of the most coherent bodies of dramatic criticism in the twentieth century, and it should be compared with and contrasted to the criticism of Yeats's countryman George Bernard Shaw.[7]

Yeats may not have believed that he could win the battle with the leaders of the commercial theatre, but he had no thought of surrender or retreat. 'Any fool can fight a winning battle,' he wrote to Lady Gregory, 'but it needs character to fight a losing one, and that should inspire us.'[8] They were inspired, and they were stubborn: 'We went on giving what we thought good until it became popular,'[9] Lady Gregory said; and she gave Yeats full credit for establishing the aesthetic premises upon which their work was based. 'I want you to sit down,' she wrote to an irresolute colleague,

> and read Mr. Yeats's notes in the last two numbers of *Samhain* and to ask yourself if the work he is doing is best worth helping or hindering. Remember, he has been for the last eight years working with his whole heart and soul for the creation, the furtherance, the perfecting, of what he believes will be a great dramatic movement in Ireland.[10]

By 1913 Yeats was convinced that his dramatic criticism was unique and enduring. 'Dear Bullen,' he wrote on 16 March,

> I have come to the conclusion that you had better start a new issue of the Collected Works with the volume of dramatic criticism; you can if you like publish the volume of Lyric poetry at the same time. The volume of dramatic criticism should, I think, contain two of Gregory's designs. The reason why I suggest it coming first is that it contains matter which has never been reviewed and never been accessible in a volume by itself. Coming at this moment when people have in their memories the Reinhardt productions, the scenery and costumes of the Russian Ballet, the Barker productions of Shakespeare — all examples of the new decorative method — it would probably get considerable attention. It would contain the only serious criticism of the new craft of the Theatre. It is the exact moment for it. (L578-79)

Whether or not it was 'the only serious criticism of the new craft,' Yeats was surely right in his assumption that it was unusual. Moreover, despite his detractors, whose numbers are steadily decreasing, it is now clear that his critical achievement as well as the plays which prompted the formulation of principles is considerable and will endure. Although I hesitate to insist that Yeats's critical writings influenced the whole of English drama, they surely were a powerful force in the new drama, on the continent and in America as well as at home.[11] The achievements of Beckett, Anouilh, Ionesco, Genet, Artaud, and Albee — to cite the first who come to mind — would not have been possible or would have been greatly different if Yeats had not suggested the way for many of their experiments. In light of his 'modernity,' it is surprising that so little attention has been given to his significance as pathfinder and leader.

Moreover, Yeats was conscious that he was an apostle of the new order. 'At the opening of a movement,' he wrote in the essay on Spenser, 'we are busy with first principles, and can find out everything but the road we are to go, everything but the weight and measure of the impulse that has to come to us out of life itself, for that is always in defiance of reason, always without a justification but by faith and works' (EI357). In the remainder of this essay, I will trace briefly the road Yeats and his collaborators were to go 'by faith and works.'

Like all proper Romantics, Yeats believed that the creation of a new order necessarily entails the destruction of the old, that the phoenix can rise only from the ashes of the dead:

> All that can be annihilated must be annihilated
> That the Children of Jerusalem may be saved from slavery.[12]

Life, he observed in 1903, 'may know its business well, but its business is building and ours is shattering';[13] '. . . only amid spiritual terror or only when all that laid hold on life is shaken can we see truth.'[14] If a writer is to be useful to his country, he must make a decisive break with the conventional past; he must destroy the self and refuse servile pandering to popular tastes. In the first issue of *Samhain* (1901), Yeats, thinking of himself as prophet, put the thought in a religious context:

Moses was little good to his people until he had killed an Egyptian; and for the most part a writer or public man of the upper classes is useless to his country till he has done something that separates him from his class. We wish to grow peaceful crops, but we must dig our furrows with the sword. (E83)

Despite his aggressive iconoclasm, Shaw had not, in Yeats's opinion, achieved that separation, perhaps because as social scientist he sought to reform the existing social and political structure rather than destroy it and build again. Yeats, in contrast, was a Romantic who was convinced that the society of his time and the art — drama, in particular — which merely reflected it were so hopelessly superficial and imitative that they must be destroyed. 'Not reformation but revelation'[15] was his ideal: 'Civilization, too, will not that also destroy where it has loved, until it shall bring the simple and natural things again, and a new Argo with all the gilding on her bows sail out to find another Fleece?' (EI290) The question is surely rhetorical.

Despite Yeats's insistence that he and his colleagues had no desire 'to reform anything' (EI300), they sought something new and different. The question was not whether they wished 'to change anything' but how they hoped to effect the change. Convinced from the beginning of his career, I suspect, 'that a man's business may at times be revelation, and not reformation' (EI103), Yeats summarized his position and suggested the underlying metaphysical assumptions in an early essay on 'The Body of the Father Christian Rosencrux':

> I cannot get it out of my mind that this age of criticism is about to pass, and an age of imagination, of emotion, of moods, of revelation, about to come in its place; for certainly belief in a supersensual world is at hand again; and when the notion that we are "phantoms of the earth and water" has gone down the wind, we will trust our own being and all it desires to invent; and when the external world is no more the standard of reality, we will learn again that the great passions are angels of God, and that to embody them "uncurbed in their eternal glory," even in their labour for the ending of man's peace and prosperity, is more than to comment, however wisely, upon the

tendencies of our time, or to express the socialistic, or humanitarian, or other forces of our time, or even "to sum up" our time, as the phrase is; for art is a revelation, and not a criticism. . . . (EI197)

Although at first glance this essay may appear to be concerned primarily with the Order of the Golden Dawn, in which Yeats was deeply involved at the time (1895), it is important to observe that his essay first appeared as part of 'a series of articles on Irish National Literature.'[16] To Yeats, as to Blake, who is quoted in the passage above, art and religion are one: 'Everything that can be seen, touched, measured, explained, understood, argued over, is to the imaginative artist nothing more than a means, for he belongs to the invisible life, and delivers its ever new and ever ancient revelation' (EI195). To the artist who lives by that credo the art object becomes a 'window into Eden,' to cite a phrase from Blake.

As a result of the Romantic conviction that you must 'Drive your cart and your plow over the bones of the dead,'[17] much of Yeats's early motivation was negative, and considerable light may be cast upon his positive theory through an examination of its negative presuppositions. He began in the optimistic assumption that he must blot out the 'London contagion,' which had changed O'Casey's 'mountain into a mouse.'[18] And the 'London contagion' was only a convenient phrase for 'what is merely commercial in the art of England' (E81). It stood for 'the general impression of vulgarity'[19] which Yeats had of almost all drama of his time, for the ideals of 'Bacon, Newton, Locke' had made most modern literature decadent.[20] Since journalists, almost without exception, were doing 'the will of the commercial theatre,'[21] abuse was 'the usual reception of intellectual drama in London' (L513); and Yeats was filled with fury when he thought of the 'authority [given] to all elements in English which create in the arts timid and conventional work' (L530). But the same might be said for the Establishment in Dublin. Writing to his father in 1915 about *Reveries over Childhood and Youth*, Yeats described the book as 'a history of the revolt, which perhaps unconsciously you taught me, against certain Victorian ideals. Dowden is the image of those ideals and has to stand for the whole structure in Dublin,

Lord Chancellors and all the rest' (L602-3).

A strong adherent of the tradition of poet as prophet, Yeats believed that all true artists are 'in protest against their time,'[22] and he set himself 'all but unwilling among those lean and fierce minds who are at war with their time, who cannot accept the days as they pass, simply and gladly' (EI50-51). Yeats knew that 'every generation is against its predecessor,' but the 'lean and fierce minds' are also the opposites of their own times.[23] 'But remember,' he wrote to A. H. Bullen in March 1908, 'that all fine artistic work is received with an outcry, with hatred even. Suspect all work that is not' (L504). And in fact Yeats protested strongly against every important dramatic trend of his day. Although he bravely insisted in April 1900 that 'We have brought the "literary drama" to Ireland, and it has become a reality,'[24] he was less optimistic three years later after the first flush of excitement had worn off: 'I think the theatre must be reformed in its plays, its speaking, its acting, and its scenery. That is to say, I think there is nothing good about it at present' (E107).

Among the writers rejected was Maeterlinck, an early idol: in a letter of 9 December 1909, Yeats described *The Blue Bird* as 'a mere libretto for the scene painter with here and there a pretentious piece of traditional poetry. It is probably another of the gasping things Maeterlinck, struggling well beyond his nature, does to please his wife. . . . I amused somebody by saying that Maeterlinck was like a little boy who has jumped up behind a taxi cab and can't get off' (L541-42). As might be expected, Yeats disapproved strongly of the innovations of Antoine. When an Irish critic suggested that the Abbey managers should 'study the stage-management of Antoine,' Yeats observed wryly, 'that is like telling a good Catholic to take his theology from Luther. Antoine, who described poetry as a way of saying nothing, has perfected naturalistic acting and carried the spirit of science into the theatre.' 'It is better,' Yeats concluded, 'to fumble our way like children' (E173). In a long and important letter to Frank Fay (28 August 1904), Yeats stated the 'position of attack' for an 'article . . . on realistic stage management.' He linked Antoine with George Moore, objecting to the theories of both on the same grounds:

Put Moore on the defensive and you will win. Be just to Antoine's genius, but show the defects of his movement. Art is art because it is not nature, and he tried to make it nature. A realist, he cared nothing for poetry, which is founded on convention. He despised it and did something to drive it from the stage. He broke up convention, we have to re-create it. . . . We must grope our way towards a new yet ancient perfection. . . . We desire an extravagant, if you will unreal, rhetorical romantic art, allied in literature to the art on the one hand of Racine and [on] the other hand of Cervantes.

Putting 'the whole business in a thimble,' Yeats concluded: 'It is the art of a theatre which knows nothing of style, nothing of magnificent words, nothing of the music of speech' (L440-41).

He was more uncertain about Ibsen, who had staunch supporters in Edward Martyn and George Moore. 'Ibsen has sincerity and logic beyond any writer of our time, and we are all seeking to learn them at his hands,' Yeats wrote; 'but is he not a good deal less than the greatest of all times, because he lacks beautiful and vivid language?' Measuring Ibsen by Blake's symbolic aesthetic, Yeats concluded that 'man has too little help from that occasional *collaborateur* [God] when he writes of people whose language has become abstract and dead' (E166). 'The root of the whole thing,' Yeats wrote in a comment on Ibsen and Sudermann, is 'the commonplace will, that is, the will of a successful business man, the business will' (L441). After attending a performance of *The Vikings at Helgeland* in 1903, Yeats expressed his doubts about Ibsen in a letter to Lady Gregory: 'I felt that Ibsen had not really grasped and unified the old life. He had no clear thought or emotion about it' (L399). Yeats had attended 'the first performance of an Ibsen play given in England,' *A Doll's House*, and recorded with obvious pleasure a remark he overheard at the end: 'It is but a series of conversations terminated by an accident' (E165). Years later, in the opening of 'The Tragic Generation,' Yeats recalled the elderly critic's observation, and then analyzed his own mingled emotions about Ibsen:

> I was divided in mind, I hated the play; what was it but Carolus Duran, Bastien-Lepage, Huxley and Tyndall all over again? I resented being invited to admire dialogue so close to modern educated speech that music and style were impossible. . . . As time passed Ibsen became in my eyes the chosen author of very clever young journalists, who, condemned to their treadmill of abstraction, hated music and style; and yet neither I nor my generation could escape him because, though we and he had not the same friends, we had the same enemies. (A279)

In effect, Yeats and his friends were forced to choose between the new drama in 'the manner of Ibsen' and the 'old-fashioned melodrama, and conventional romance' (A280). The school of Ibsen was merely the lesser of two evils. Yeats read his collected works in the Archer translation, and admired Florence Farr in several of the plays, notably *Rosmersholm*, 'where there is symbolism and a stale odour of spilt poetry' (A280). Yeats admired the man apparently, but disliked the work he had made popular, especially the problem plays.

They, of course, were much to be preferred over the well-made plays in the French tradition of Scribe which offers, Yeats concluded, 'nothing . . . that has not succeeded a thousand times before the curtain has risen. . . . The whole movement of theatrical reform in our day has been a struggle to get rid of this kind of play, and the sincere play, the logical play, that we would have in its place, will always seem, when we hear it for the first time, undramatic, unexciting.'[25] 'The modern theatre,' he observed, 'has died away to what it is because the writers have thought of their audiences instead of their subject' (E164). He usually described the well-made play and its descendents as 'the play of modern manners,' which he analyzed with some care in 'Discoveries':

> Of all artistic forms that have had a large share of the world's attention, the worst is the play about modern educated people. Except where it is superficial or deliberately argumentative it fills one's soul with a sense of commonness as with dust. It has one mortal ailment. It cannot become impassioned, that is to

say, vital, without making somebody gushing and sentimental. Educated and well-bred people do not wear their hearts upon their sleeves, and they have no artistic and charming language except light persiflage and no powerful language at all, and when they are deeply moved they look silently into the fireplace. . . . Ibsen understood the difficulty and made all his characters a little provincial that they might not put each other out of countenance, and made a leading-article sort of poetry — phrases about vine-leaves and harps in the air. . . . It was certainly an understanding of the slightness of the form, of its incapacity for the expression of the deeper sorts of passion, that made the French invent the play with a thesis, for where there is a thesis people can grow hot in argument, almost the only kind of passion that displays itself in our daily life. (EI274-75)

Although Yeats emphasized the 'meagre language' and the 'action crushed into the narrow limits of possibility,' (EI275) he disliked everything about 'the play of modern manners.' 'I come always back to this thought,' he said; 'there is something of an old wives' tale in fine literature' (EI276). The modern play is concerned with surface conditions. It has no extravagance, never probes the depth of the mind. 'I cannot explain it,' Yeats concluded, 'but I am certain that every high thing was invented in this way, between sleeping and waking, as it were, and that peering and peeping persons are but hawkers of stolen goods. How else could their noses have grown so ravenous or their eyes so sharp?' (EI277)

One could go on indefinitely quoting Yeats's railleries at contemporary stage conventions. Fundamentally, I think, his objections were religious: he was firmly convinced that the loss of faith in man had destroyed fine literature. 'This change,' he said, with Ibsen's 'intellectual drama of real life' in mind, 'coincided with the substitution of science for religion in the conduct of life, and is, I believe, as temporary, for the practice of twenty centuries will surely take the sway in the end' (E195). 'The more religious the subject-matter of an art,' he wrote, 'the more will it be as it were, stationary, and the more ancient will be the emotion that it arouses and the circumstance that it calls up before our eyes' (EI285). Such arguments for art as religion are the basis for Yeats's symbolic aesthetic. All things here are temporary. Hence, 'it is impossible to separate our idea of what is noble from a mystic stair' — that is, in a phrase from an unpublished essay on magic, 'a ladder into heaven.' The tide of the time was factual and scientific, its so-called progress 'too modern and momentary to endure.' But Yeats had faith: 'All art is dream, and what the day is done with is dreaming-ripe, and what art has moulded religion accepts, and in the end all is in the wine-cup, all is in the drunken fantasy, and the grapes begin to stammer' (EI285). Yeats found a sentence in Blake's *Marriage of Heaven and Hell* to illustrate his belief that all great art is symbolic and religious, based upon a 'system of correspondences' relating the visible world to the invisible: 'The best wine is the oldest, the best water is the newest.' The wine suggested to Yeats the emotion and 'drunken fantasy' of the Eleusinian Mysteries, and the water suggested 'experience, immediate sensation' (EI284). He was, I suspect, recalling that water was a common Neoplatonic symbol for the material world. ('What's water but the generated soul?') It is important to point out in this context that Yeats's remarkably subtle argument is primarily concerned with 'The Subject-Matter of Drama.' Yeats wanted the arts to 'grow serious as the Ten Commandments' (EI99), and he expected the drama to be the means of preparing the 'priesthood [which] will spread their religion everywhere, and make their Art the Art of the people' (EI167-68).

But he concluded that 'the world is not old enough to show us any example' (EI168), and in fact when he thought about the examples of history he was inclined to be pessimistic: 'Somebody has said that every nation begins with poetry and ends with algebra, and passion has always refused to express itself in algebraical terms' (E167-68). Although he consoled himself with the knowledge that history is cyclical, he was convinced that 'the ill-breeding and theatricality of Carlyle . . . [and] the magniloquence of Hugo . . . belong to an industrial age, a mechanical sequence of ideas' (EI236). The mathematical contagion had spread to all art, but drama had suffered most, perhaps because it was pre-eminently an art of the people:

> It is only the writers of our modern dramatic movement, our scientific dramatists, our naturalists of the stage, who have thought it possible to be like the greatest, and yet to cast aside even the poor persiflage of the comedians, and to write in the impersonal language that has come, not out of individual life, nor out of life at all, but out of necessities of commerce, of Parliament, of Board Schools, of hurried journeys by rail. . . . One must not forget that the death of language, the substitution of phrases as nearly impersonal as algebra for words and rhythms varying from man to man, is but part of the tyranny of impersonal things. (EI301)

In Yeats's thinking the dramatists of his time no longer sought 'to express hopes and alarms common to every man that ever came into the world, but politics or social passion, a veiled or open propaganda' (EI301-2). 'Contemporary drama,' he concluded, 'knows of little else' than 'the business will in a high state of activity' (EI177); it had become 'the machine-shop of the realists' (EI267) for the mass production of 'the literature of the point of view,' which, Yeats said in 1937, 'I hated and still hate with an ever growing hatred' (EI511). 'My generation,' he recalled, 'because it disliked Victorian rhetorical fervour, came to dislike all rhetoric' (EI497).

That observation was made in 1936, but Yeats knew from the beginning that rhetoric was simply 'the will trying to do the work of the imagination' (EI215), for he had learned from William Blake that art cannot flourish in 'mathematic form' projected on the 'wheels and pulleys necessary to the effect' (EI238): 'Art bids us touch and taste and hear and see the world, and shrinks from what Blake calls mathematic form, from every abstract thing, from all that is of the brain only, from all that is not a fountain jetting from the entire hopes, memories, and sensations of the body. Its morality is personal, knows little of any general law . . .' (EI292-93).

To Yeats, of course, the emphasis on the 'wheels and pulleys' in the 'theatre of commerce' was the inevitable outgrowth of an industrial society which put its whole trust in science and believed that the conquest of nature and clearance of slums represented progress. 'The scientific movement,' he wrote in 1900, 'brought with it a literature which was always tending to lose itself in externalities of all kinds, in opinion, in declamation, in picturesque writing, in word painting, or in what Mr. Symons has called an attempt "to build in brick and mortar inside the covers of a book"' (EI155). Even the singer in a play 'seems no longer a human being but an invention of science'; as a result, Yeats wrote, 'I am bored and wretched, a limitation I greatly regret.'[26] If Yeats knew Elmer Rice's *Adding Machine*, he surely considered it the ironic fulfilment of his prophecy.

From the beginning of his career apparently Yeats saw clearly that a machine civilization emphasizing progress through mass production was destructive of the arts. 'When I was a boy,' he wrote in the introduction to *The Resurrection*, 'everybody talked about progress, and rebellion against my elders took the form of aversion to that myth' (E392). The city itself, and London in particular, reflected the popular faith in this theory, and realistic urban literature 'created for the common people' (EI227) was a direct outgrowth. 'In London,' as Yeats phrased it, 'where all the intellectual traditions gather to die, men hate a play if they are told it is literature, for they will not endure a spiritual superiority. . . .'[27] As they became increasingly absorbed in the 'wheels and pulleys,' theatre managers put the mind of the audience to sleep with 'meretricious landscapes' and magnificent costumes, and 'gradually perfected the theatre of commerce, the masterpiece of that movement towards externality in life and thought and art against which the criticism of our day is learning to protest' (EI169). Yeats was certain that 'An Englishman, with his belief in progress, with his instinctive preference for the cosmopolitan literature of the last century, may think arts like these parochial, but they are the arts we have begun the making of' (EI206). It was time, Yeats thought, to 'press the popular arts on to a more complete realism . . . for the commercial arts demoralise by their compromise, their incompleteness, their idealism without sincerity or elegance, their pretence that ignorance can understand beauty' (EI228). Thinking in Platonic terms, Yeats related reality to the 'world of imagination,' to the spiritual not the physical realm. To him, 'all life is revelation beginning in miracle and enthusiasm, and dying out as it unfolds itself in what we have mistaken for progress' (EI171). But life is revelation only to the artist, whose business is neither criticism (EI197) nor reformation (EI103). Reality, the truth about man's existence, is not factual, not to be apprehended through observation of nature. The artist comprehends the 'more complete realism' in a visionary flash and projects it as a 'window into Eden.' Like Blake and the followers of Plato, Yeats insisted that 'Progress is miracle, and it is sudden, because miracles are the work of an all-powerful energy, and Nature in herself has no power except to die and to forget' (EI172). As Blake said, in the fundamental epistemological assumption of the symbolist artist, 'Nature has no Supernatural & dissolves: Imagination is Eternity' (B779); and Yeats was quite as certain as Blake that 'Where man is not, nature is barren' (B152). 'If we poets are to move the people,' Yeats decided, 'we must reintegrate the human spirit in our imagination' (EI264).

For many years of his life Yeats devoted all his active energy to the achievement of this reintegration through the drama, which he considered 'the most immediately powerful form of literature, the most vivid image of life' (E119). Realizing early that every generation must oppose its predecessor (EI417) and that 'you cannot have health among a people if you have not prophet, priest and king' (EI264), Yeats sought to overthrow 'those enemies of life, the chimeras of the Pulpit and the Press' (E119) through a complete reformation of the theatre (E107). He was not foolishly optimistic, recognizing as early as 1899 certainly that 'It will take a generation, and perhaps generations, to restore the theatre of art; for one must get one's actors, and perhaps one's scenery, from the theatre of commerce, until new actors and new painters have come to help one; and until many failures and imperfect successes have made a new tradition, and perfected in detail the ideal that is beginning to float before our eyes' (EI170). Sometimes even he could suggest that 'we who are the opposites of our times should for the most part work at our art and for good manners' sake be silent' (E417). But this was said in retrospect, and all students of drama are surely grateful that he was not silent, that in fact he produced what may well prove to be the most significant body of dramatic criticism in our time.

Much of it is practical, springing directly from day-to-day observations of production in the Abbey Theatre and concerning itself chiefly with acting, scenery, staging, costuming, etc. More significant, however, is the criticism concerned with philosophical assumptions about the nature of man and art as they bear directly on the drama.

'All that can be annihilated must be annihilated,' but once the old building has been destroyed, the new one must be built. Reflecting upon 'the decline of spiritual and intellectual energies,' Yeats suggested that 'it should be our business to bring Ireland from under the ruins.'[28] He erected his structure upon a Romantic epistemology: 'Descartes, Locke, and Newton took away the world and gave us its excrement instead. Berkeley restored the world. . . . Berkeley has brought back to us the world that only exists because it shines and sounds' (E325). Turning back to Berkeleyan idealism enabled Yeats to develop a logically consistent aesthetic within which he could fit almost all the elements of his dramatic theory and practice. A brief essay in 'Pages from a Diary in 1930' suggests the basic premises upon which his doctrine of art rests:

> I would found literature on the three things which Kant thought we must postulate to make life livable — Freedom, God, Immortality. The fading of these three before "Bacon, Newton, Locke" has made literature decadent. Because Freedom is gone we have Stendhal's "mirror dawdling down a lane"; because God has gone we have realism, the accidental, because Immortality is gone we can no longer write those tragedies which have always seemed to me alone legitimate — those that are a joy to the man who dies. Recent Irish literature has only delighted me in so far as it implies one or the other, in so far as it has been a defiance of all else. . . .[29]

This passage is primarily important in pointing out the deleterious effects of eighteenth-century epistemology and cosmology. Man has no freedom of action because he comes into the world with a pure white blank for a mind and can therefore know only what he observes in nature, which operates predictably under a set of absolute and unvarying laws. The artist can merely copy nature, and he sees all life as an accident because man has no control over his environment. If man's actions have no dignity because he is a mere pawn, the artist can have no joy in creation because he sees no abiding purpose in existence, no permanence in the physical world. There can be no tragic joy if the protagonist and his creator do not find purpose through belief in the life to come — if he cannot believe, as Blake put it, that 'Time is the Mercy of Eternity; without Time's swiftness / . . . all were eternal torment' (B510). The symbolic artist 'can isolate the human mind and its vices as if in eternity' (E333). That is, he transcends the limitations of time and space: the art object is a 'vision of eternity.' Out of this Romantic revolt grew the aesthetic faith upon which the Irish Renaissance was founded. As Yeats pointed out, 'The movement began with Æ's first little verses made out of the Upanishads, and my *Celtic Twilight*, a bit of ornamental trivial needlework sewn on a prophetic fury got by Blake and Boehme' (E333). Although he was to decide in time that spirituality could be achieved without the vague indefiniteness of such work as the *Celtic Twilight*, Yeats never lost the Platonic conviction that time is merely a pale reflection of eternity, and upon that faith he founded a theory of symbolism which was quite as necessary to the plays as to the lyric poems.

He based his theory of symbolism on the Romantic assumption, originating with Plato, that 'Man Brings All that he has or can have Into the World with him. Man is Born Like a Garden ready Planted & Sown' because 'This World is too poor to produce one Seed.'[30] And why is this world unproductive? Simply because it is merely a pale reflex of the ideal world, a 'delusion of Ulro,' as Blake called it, and in fact does not exist at all. As Yeats once said of Shakespeare, 'He meditated as Solomon, not as Bentham meditated, upon blind ambitions, untoward accidents, and capricious passions, and the world was almost as empty in his eyes as it must be in the eyes of God' (EI106-7). For the man of vision, however, the earth serves an indispensable function as the symbolic image of the ideal world: only through the imperfect copy can we get a glimpse of Eden. According to 'the great magical precept of Hermes Trismegistus,' which is the metaphysical basis for Yeats's religion and theory of symbolism, 'That which is below is like that which is above, and that which is above is like that which is below, for the performance of the miracles of the one substance.' 'This is,' in the words of Yeats's friend MacGregor Mathers, 'the fundamental principle of all the ancient mystic doctrines, whether qabalistical, mythological, alchemical, or magical. . . . As Macrocosm, so Microcosm; as eternity, so life!'[31] Yeats surely agreed.

Many of his most striking critical comments about drama and most of his own plays reflect in one way or another this basic symbolic assumption. Out of this faith came Yeats's preoccupation with the 'great tradition,' for no other was worthwhile:

> Every writer, even every small writer, who has belonged to the great tradition, has had his dream of an impossibly noble life, and the greater he is, the more does it seem to plunge him into some beautiful or bitter reverie. Some, and of these are all the earliest poets of the world, gave it direct expression; others mingle it so subtly with reality that it is a day's work to disentangle it; others bring it near by showing us whatever is most its contrary. (EI303-4)

Among these last is Synge, who 'sets before us ugly, deformed or sinful people, but his people, moved by no practical ambition, are driven by a dream of that impossible life' (EI304).

More directly to the point perhaps is Yeats's comment on *The Well of the Saints*: 'He tells us of realities, but he knows that art has never taken more than its symbols from anything that the eye can see or the hand measure' (EI304). Art, Yeats wrote in the essay on Shakespeare, 'brings us near to the archetypal ideas themselves, and away from nature, which is but their looking-glass' (EI102). During the rehearsals for *The Well of the Saints*, Yeats summarized an aesthetic principle for the production which might be applied to his own plays: 'For though the people of the play use no phrase they could not use in daily life, we know that we are seeking to express what no eye has ever seen' (EI305). If it is to have an abiding influence, literature 'will measure all things by the measure not of things visible but of things invisible' (E161). The function of the real, then, is merely to suggest the unreal, though Yeats would not have phrased it that way, preferring to use such terms as 'spiritual reality' or 'more complete realism.' 'Repelled by what had seemed the sole reality,' he recalled in the Introduction to *Fighting the Waves*, 'we had returned to romantic dreaming, to the nobility of tradition' (E372).

Once Yeats decided that the unseen world of the imagination was 'the real & eternal World of which this Vegetable Universe is but a faint shadow' (B717), he developed little by little in criticism and practice a dramatic theory to support what well may have been at first merely a revolt against crass materialism and false emotion. If art is not to copy nature but the ideal model upon which nature is patterned, the artist obviously must avoid realism, and if he is consistent he must search for an organic vehicle by means of which he can suggest not this world but the ideal world beyond. In Yeats's words, 'All imaginative art remains at a distance and this distance, once chosen, must be firmly held against a pushing world' (EI224). The theory is attractive, but problems remain. First, obviously, is how far to set the distance. Yeats realized that the distance must be great enough to 'enable us to pass for a few moments into a deep of the mind that had hitherto been too subtle for our habitation' (EI225), but not so far that the symbolic projection of the vision will not speak for itself. Yeats, as usual, was aware of the difficulty. 'To put it otherwise,' he wrote in 'Discoveries,'

> We should ascend out of common interests, the thoughts of the newspapers, of the market-place, of men of science, but only so far as we can carry the normal, passionate, reasoning self, the personality as a whole. We must find some place upon the Tree of Life for the phoenix' nest, for the passion that is exaltation and the negation of the will, for the wings that are always upon fire, set high that the forked branches may keep it safe, yet low enough to be out of the little wind-tossed boughs, the quivering of the twigs. (EI272)

In part at least the search for the proper distance is projected in the search for a style, and all students who have read the plays chronologically know that Yeats's aesthetic quest for the ideal psychic distance was never ended — a fact which has much to do with our continuing interest in him as a dramatic critic.

But the art of the theatre encompasses many arts, and if the artist is to hold the door against the pushing world, he must find a means of combining these various arts in some organic union to establish and maintain the ideal psychic barrier which the artist strives for. Yeats was acutely aware of the problem:

> Verse, ritual, music, and dance in association with action require that gesture, costume, facial expression, stage arrangement must help in keeping the door. Our unimaginative arts are content to set a piece of the world as we know it in a place by itself, to put their photographs as it were in a plush or a plain frame, but the arts which interest me, while seeming to separate from the world and us a group of figures, images, symbols, enable us to pass for a few moments into a deep of the mind that had hitherto been too subtle for our habitation. (EI224-25)

To realize this ideal union, Yeats concluded, 'we should distrust bodily distance, mechanism, and loud noise' (EI225); and to achieve the ideal implied in this distrust, Yeats proposed to reform the theatre 'in its plays, its speaking, its acting, and its scenery' (E107).

In 'The Reform of the Theatre' (*Samhain*, 1903), Yeats made specific suggestions for the commercial theatre, about which 'there is nothing good . . . at present.' '*First*,' he said, 'we have to write or find plays that will make the theatre a place of intellectual excitement — a place where the mind goes to be liberated as it was liberated by the theatres of Greece and England and France at certain great moments of their history, and as it is liberated in Scandinavia to-day' (E107). If such plays were to be successful, in Yeats's judgment, both writers and audiences must develop 'a stronger feeling for beautiful and appropriate language than one finds in the ordinary theatre,' for there is in fact, 'nothing immortal in literature except style' (E107). The first of Yeats's specific proposals, therefore, was 'to restore words to their sovereignty . . . [to] make speech even more important than gesture upon the stage.' Next in importance was to 'simplify acting, especially in poetical drama, and in prose drama that is remote from real life like my *Hour-Glass*.' Finally, he wrote, 'just as it is necessary to simplify gesture that it may accompany speech without being its rival, it is necessary to simplify both the form and colour of scenery and costume' (E108-9).

It is not, I hope, emphasizing the obvious to point out that these practical ideals spring directly from and are completely consonant with the aesthetic ideal of the symbolic play designed as a single lyric emotion to project the poet's 'cry for a more abundant and a more intense life'[32] in contrast to what Yeats called the 'magnificent hysteria' of plays like *Mrs. Tanqueray*.[33]

If the artist was to project 'the rich, far-wandering, many-imaged life of the half-seen world beyond' (EI216), his productions must avoid copying realistic commonplaces, which are after all delusory; and they should suggest the spiritual reality of the ideal world. Insisting that 'the intellect of Ireland is romantic and spiritual rather than scientific and analytical'[34] and recognizing that 'the theatre began in ritual' (EI170), Yeats decided that 'we must . . . take upon ourselves the method and the fervour of a priesthood' (EI203), and that 'our plays will be for the most part remote, spiritual, and ideal' (EI166). 'As a reader for the Abbey Theatre,' Yeats once said, 'I have learnt much of Ireland . . . , perhaps as much as a priest learns in the confessional' (E445).

But how was the dramatist to 'restore words to their ancient sovereignty'? Attractive as it sounds, what does such phraseology mean? What action does it suggest? Several things are implied. Most important perhaps are the religious overtones: '. . . I never hear the vivid, picturesque, ever-varied language of Mr. Synge's persons,' Yeats wrote, 'without feeling that the great *collaborateur* has his finger in our business.'[35] But 'is it possible to make a work of art, which needs every subtlety of expression if it is to reveal what hides itself continually, out of a dying, or at any rate a very ailing, language?' (E167) Only if the poet turns back to 'the common life, where language is as much alive as if it were new come out of Eden.' In fact all language except 'that of the poets and the poor is already bed-ridden' (E167). Hence the concentration on peasant and aristocrat: one had never lost the vision of Eden, the other had found it through wisdom. The language must be vibrant and concrete with the emphasis entirely on the spoken word: 'I have spent my life,'

Yeats remarked as he approached its end, 'in clearing out of poetry every phrase written for the eye, and bringing all back to syntax that is for ear alone. . . . As I altered my syntax I altered my intellect' (EI529-30). In 1937, when he made that profound observation, he was still searching for syntax and words to express 'character in action' rather than 'action in character.' It should be observed perhaps that the continuing search for an appropriate style was related in Yeats's mind to the quest for innocence — the 'vision of Eden,' as he once called it: '. . . as we are encouraged to believe that our intellects grow with our years,' he wrote to Ashe King (in May 1925), 'I may be permitted the conviction that — grown a little nearer innocence — I have found a more appropriate simplicity.'[36]

Even more striking as a theory of language may be Yeats's conception that the words themselves, their movement in the sentence, and their total relationship in the completed work of art should strive to image their divine origin by projecting a vision of the life beyond. In Yeats's mind, Synge 'made word and phrase dance to a very strange rhythm' which 'perfectly fits the drifting emotion, the dreaminess, the vague yet measureless desire, for which he would create a dramatic form.' That is, both words and syntax embody in their imaginative reality the organic rhythm of the universe. As a result, Synge's rhythm 'blurs definition, clear edges, everything that comes from the will, it turns imagination from all that is of the present, like a gold background in a religious picture, and it strengthens in every emotion whatever comes to it from far off, from brooding memory and dangerous hope' (EI299-300). In the apprehension of ideal reality this universal rhythm urges the mind of the artist to the edge of trance, and he projects his vision in the form of a ritual in worship of the life force. Since the motion of the artist's mind reflects that of the *anima mundi* rather than the phenomenal world, the movement of the language will follow the meditative movement of the mind: 'In all drama which would give direct expression to reverie, to the speech of the soul with itself, there is some device that checks the rapidity of the dialogue' (EI333). The direct result of this theory was an attempt to train the actors to rid their speech of 'accidental variety' (L451). Both the words and their rhythmic patterns must not only suggest eternal values but also symbolize eternity itself. In the most successful plays, Yeats could imagine the characters passing 'by as before an open window, murmuring strange, exciting words.'[37]

The effect of words which image the world beyond will, of course, be lost if the actions on the stage copy those of the busy world outside. In 1937, as he wrote a proposed 'Introduction for My Plays,' Yeats sought to recall the aesthetic impulses which prompted him to write, produce, and analyze plays:

> When I follow back my stream to its source I find two dominant desires: I wanted to get rid of irrelevant movement — the stage must become still that words might keep all their vividness — and I wanted vivid words. When I saw a London play, I saw actors crossing the stage not because the play compelled them, but because a producer said they must do so to keep the attention of the audience; and I heard words that had no vividness except what they borrowed from the situation. It seems that I was confirmed in this idea or I found it when I first saw Sarah Bernhardt play in *Phèdre*, and that it was I who converted the players, but I am old, I must have many false memories; perhaps I was Synge's convert. It was certainly a day of triumph when the first act of *The Well of the Saints* held its audience, though the two chief persons sat side by side under a stone cross from start to finish. This rejection of all needless movement first drew the attention of critics. The players still try to preserve it, though audiences accustomed to the cinema expect constant change. . . . (EI527-28)

Over-generous as usual in giving credit to his colleagues, Yeats recalled that Frank Fay had agreed with him, though Fay 'sometimes loved' the flourishes and the rhetoric of 'the existing conventions of the theatre.' Nevertheless, Yeats added nostalgically, 'were he living now and both of us young, I would ask his help to elaborate new conventions in writing and representation' (EI529). Of course, these observations were made long after the fact, and Yeats may indeed have had 'many false memories.' After several years of experimentation with the tradition of the Noh plays, he may be unintentionally exaggerating the emphasis he had placed upon 'marmorean stillness' (EI255). It should be pointed out, however, that he had insisted almost from the beginning that 'we must get rid of everything that is restless' (E109). When this was written (1903), Yeats sought to eliminate 'irrelevant movement' in order not to draw the attention of the audience away from 'vivid words' and 'the sound of the voice' (E109). By 1937, however, he was less certain which of his two 'dominant desires' should receive priority. Even in *The Well of the Saints*, he decided, 'there are scenes . . . which seem to me over-rich in words because the realistic action does not permit that stilling and slowing which turns the imagination in upon itself' (EI529). Yeats must have had difficulty restricting the movement on the stage of actors trained in the melodramatic tradition. He recalled that he had insisted that Frank Fay carry 'a spear instead of a sword because I knew that he would flourish a sword in imitation of an actor in an eighteenth-century engraving' (EI528). In 1916, during the rehearsals of *At the Hawk's Well*, Yeats was forced to stronger measures to control the musician and the actor who played Cuchulain. Writing to Lady Gregory (on 28 March) that 'I believe I have at last found a dramatic form that suits me,' Yeats described his problems with the cast:

> The play goes on well except for Ainley, who waves his arms like a drowning kitten, and the musician, who is in a constant rage. She says "in the big London theatres the action is stopped from time to time to give the musician his turn." I am going this afternoon to Dulac's to go on working out gestures for Ainley. They are then to be all drawn by Dulac. (L609-10)

Although Yeats's aversion to excessive movements and rhetorical flourishes was based upon sound aesthetic convictions derived from the pre-Raphaelites, he justified his innovations on a religious base as well: 'Ritual, the most powerful form of drama, differs from the ordinary form, because everyone who hears it is also a player' (E129). Although Yeats was here referring to the Greek drama, his concern with ritual was strongly influenced by the rites and ceremonies of the Golden Dawn. He had served as Imperator and as Instructor in

Mystical Philosophy, and he had helped compose and revise at least some of the rituals.[38] When he insisted that 'the theatre of art . . . must therefore discover grave and decorative gestures,' he was surely mindful of the precise symbolic movements in the ritualistic ceremonies of the Golden Dawn. Indeed, his interest in drama, certainly the emphasis he placed upon its religious origin, was stimulated by involvement in an Order founded upon the Hermetic cosmology: 'For things below are copies, the Great Smaragdine Tablet said.'[39] All its rituals, copies of which are preserved in his papers,[40] are stylized dramas, as Kathleen Raine points out:

> The rituals and ceremonies, with their figures of Egyptian gods, Horus, Osiris and Isis, who speak through masks as from some super-human state of being and knowledge, bear a striking resemblance, in this respect, to Yeats's "drama of the soul". The idea that in religious ceremonial the gods themselves speak from a super-human world is old and universal. . . .[41]

'The theatre began in ritual,' Yeats wrote in 1899, at a time when he was deeply involved in the affairs of the Golden Dawn, 'and it cannot come to its greatness again without recalling words to their ancient sovereignty' (EI170). Years later, in 1931, he concluded the Introduction to *The Words upon the Window-Pane*, his most successful spiritualistic drama, with an observation about the relationship of the visible world to the invisible which suggests the extent of his debt to the Hermetic tradition: 'All about us there seems to start up a precise inexplicable teeming life, and the earth becomes once more, not in rhetorical metaphor, but in reality, sacred.'[42]

But the attempt to hold off the pushing world by vivid language and ritualistic movement would be futile in a setting which did not establish the remoteness and distance of the ideal world, so Yeats devoted considerable energy and time to properly simple and suggestive backgrounds. 'Illusion,' he said, 'is impossible, and should not be attempted' (EI78). Moreover, 'Naturalistic scene-painting is not an art, but a trade, because it is, at best, an attempt to copy the more obvious effects of Nature by the methods of the ordinary landscape-painter, and by his methods made coarse and summary' (EI100).

What he wanted is less clear than what he wanted to avoid, but the principle is stated repeatedly, and it is clear that the primary function of the simplified scenery was auxiliary — that is, to help the holy word recover its ancient sovereignty. 'I have simplified scenery,' he reflected in 1916, 'having *The Hour-Glass*, for instance, played now before green curtains, now among those admirable ivory-coloured screens invented by Gordon Craig. With every simplification the voice has recovered something of its importance.' 'For nearly three centuries,' by Yeats's estimate, 'invention has been making the human voice and the movements of the body seem always less expressive.' Even the singer 'seems no longer a human being but an invention of science' (EI222-23). Every artist must choose the distance best suited to suggest the proper 'remoteness and ideality' for his personal vision, and the distance will vary from artist to artist according to the medium he selects. But 'having chosen the distance from naturalism which will keep one's composition from competing with the illusion created by the actor, who belongs to a world with depth as well as height and breadth, one must keep this distance without flinching' (E178). Few playwrights and almost no stage designers of the time met Yeats's expectations. Gordon Craig was a notable exception. Yeats considered his designs for a Purcell Society performance as 'the first beautiful scenery our stage has seen. He created an ideal country where everything was possible, even speaking in verse, or speaking to music, or the expression of the whole of life in a dance.' Craig had achieved the ideal distance in a 'purple back-cloth that made Dido and Aeneas seem wandering on the edge of eternity.' Art, Yeats observed, with Craig's designs in mind, 'brings us near to the archetypal ideas themselves, and away from nature, which is but their looking-glass' (EI100-2). That may not be a just evaluation of Craig's intention or achievement, but it is a strikingly appropriate description of Yeats's metaphysic and aesthetic.

The costumes and scenery likewise must hold off the busy, pushing world and project the life beyond. His observations about the production of George Russell's *Deirdre* will illustrate:

> I thought the costumes and scenery, which were designed by Æ himself, good, too, though I did not think them simple enough.

They were more simple than ordinary stage costumes and scenery, but I would like to see poetical drama, which tries to keep at a distance from daily life that it may keep its emotion untroubled, staged with but two or three colours. The background, especially in small theatres, where its form is broken up and lost when the stage is at all crowded, should, I think, be thought out as one thinks out the background of a portrait. One often needs nothing more than a single colour, with perhaps a few shadowy forms to suggest wood or mountain. (E88)

Especially important to a study of Yeats's theory of the theatre is a letter of 27 January 1899 to the Editor of the *Daily Chronicle*. Yeats's letter was in effect a commentary upon a controversy between George Moore and William Archer, who had reviewed *The Heather Field* in the *Chronicle*. To Archer's opinion that 'the whole mounting' of Yeats's *Countess Cathleen* 'should be . . . elaborate and rich' Moore had replied that 'Mr. Yeats would have the play performed without scenery and without costumes.' Although Yeats was closer to Moore than Archer, he disagreed with both:

> . . . I see in my imagination a stage where there shall be both scenery and costumes, but scenery and costumes which will draw little attention to themselves and cost little money. I have noticed at a rehearsal how the modern coats and the litter on the stage draw one's attention, and baffle the evocation, which needs all one's thought. . . . I have noticed, too, how elaborate costumes and scenery silence the evocation completely, and substitute the cheap effects of a dressmaker and of a meretricious painter for an imaginative glory. I would have such costumes as would not disturb my imagination by staring anachronism or irrelevant splendour, and such scenery as would be forgotten the moment a good actor had said, "The dew is falling," or "I can hear the wind among the leaves." . . . I want to be able to forget everything in the real world, in watching an imaginative glory. (L308-9)

The remainder of Yeats's remarkable letter is a sustained defence of his labour 'to awaken again our interests in the moral and spiritual realities which were once the foundation of the arts' (L310). Yeats remained firmly convinced that scenery and costumes must be simple and timeless,[43] but his associates at the Abbey did not always agree. '[Fay] is anxious about the scenery,' Yeats wrote to Lady Gregory on 21 January 1904, 'and I have written to Miss Horniman suggesting as delicately as I could that there ought not to be gorgeousness of costume' (L427). As the 'good angel' of the Abbey, Miss Horniman obviously required special treatment.

An enthusiastic letter to Charles Ricketts some ten years later (11 June 1914) will illustrate how important every detail of the production was to Yeats in the achievement of unity of desired effect:

> I think the costumes the best stage costumes I have ever seen. They are full of dramatic invention, and yet nothing starts out, or seems eccentric. The Company never did the play so well, and such is the effect of costume that whole scenes got a new intensity, and passages or actions that had seemed commonplace became powerful and moving. (L587)

An early observation about setting to Fiona Macleod (William Sharp) suggests that Yeats conceived his plays from the beginning as symbolic, ritualistic, and religious:

> My own theory of poetical or legendary drama is that it should have no realistic, or elaborate, but only a symbolic and decorative setting. A forest, for instance, should be represented by a forest pattern and not by a forest painting. One should design a scene which would be an accompaniment not a reflection of the text. . . .[44] The acting should have an equivalent distance to that of the play from common realities. The plays might be almost, in some cases, modern mystery plays. (L280)

At this time, 1897, before his practical experience in the theatre, Yeats perhaps wanted all his plays to be 'magical and mystical,' as he described *The Shadowy Waters*. The influence of the Golden Dawn was especially strong.

Although Yeats knew less of acting than of the other arts which had a part in his symbolic drama, he was certain that the acting like the subject matter should maintain an appropriate distance from 'common realities' (L280). Though he admitted to Frank Fay in 1902 that he 'really did not feel competent' to criticize the acting, he did not hesitate to tell Fay what he thought:

> In two or three years I shall understand the subject but I don't yet. I know that all the acting of verse that I have seen up to this has been wrong, and I can see that you and your brother have struck out a method that would be right for verse, but, till I have seen that method applied by many different people, I will only be able to criticize acting very vaguely.... Two years ago I was in the same state about scenery that I now am in about acting. I knew the right principles but I did not know the right practice because I had never seen it. I have now however learnt a great deal from Gordon Craig. (L371)

Confident as usual that he knew the 'right principles,' Yeats only needed to experiment. Consistent with his aesthetic premises concerning the perfect union of the arts which the theatre represented, Yeats began with the assumption that acting must be restored to the ancient simplicity of a time when 'the players understood that their art was essentially conventional, artificial, ceremonious.' Above all, they must not weary the mind 'with any but the most needful changes of pitch or note, or by an irrelevant or obtrusive gesture' (E172). In order to project the impression that he stands 'at the trysting-place of mortal and immortal, time and eternity,' the actor must achieve 'marmorean stillness' in imitation of the life beyond rather than that of the chaotic, busy life outside the theatre. In 'Certain Noble Plays of Japan' (April 1916), Yeats expressed a desire that 'the player who will speak the part of Cuchulain [in *At the Hawk's Well*] . . . will appear perhaps like an image seen in reverie by some Orphic worshipper.' 'I hope,' he added, 'to have attained the distance from life which can make credible strange events, elaborate words. . . . Instead of the players working themselves into a violence of passion indecorous in our sitting-room, the music, the beauty of form and voice all come to climax in pantomimic dance.' Cuchulain was to wear a mask and head-dress Yeats described as 'this noble, half-Greek, half-Asiatic face' (EI221). By 1916 he had decided that

> A mask will enable me to substitute for the face of some commonplace player, or for that face repainted to suit his own vulgar fancy, the fine invention of a sculptor, and to bring the audience close enough to the play to hear every inflection of the voice. A mask never seems but a dirty face, and no matter how close you go is yet a work of art; nor shall we lose by stilling the movement of the features, for deep feeling is expressed by a movement of the whole body.[45]

The most exciting suggestion in this passage is, I think, the parallel drawn between sculpture and drama. As most students of Yeats know, the influence of this analogy became pervasive and increasingly important in his poetry as well as drama. In order to project 'a moment of intense life, an action . . . taken out of all other actions, . . . the dramatist must picture life in action, with an unpreoccupied mind, as the musician pictures it in sound and the sculptor in form' (E153-54). Here, as always, Yeats sought to contrast the movement of time to the stillness of eternity, and his aesthetic theory was based upon a metaphysical or religious conviction. One sentence from 'The Subject-Matter of Drama' in 'Discoveries' will illustrate: 'The more religious the subject-matter of an art, the more will it be, as it were, stationary, and the more ancient will be the emotion that it arouses and the circumstances that it calls up before our eyes' (EI285). As concrete example, Yeats cites a pilgrimage to 'the cave of vision' in Saint Patrick's Purgatory.

It is important to keep in mind that although Yeats continued to expand and develop his theory of the theatre as a result of years of experimenting at both writing and producing, the fundamental aesthetic remained unchanged. Everything must be subordinate to speech. 'I have been the advocate of the poetry as against the actor,' Yeats said, 'but I am the advocate of the actor as against the scenery' (E177). Desiring above all that 'the actors [be] kept still enough to give poetical writing its full effect upon the stage,' he 'had once asked a dramatic company to let me rehearse them in barrels that they might forget gesture and have their minds free to think of speech for a while' (E86). He wanted the actors to focus their minds upon and order their movements by a dream of the 'Unseen Life,'[46] and he was explicit in both theory and direction:

> That we may throw emphasis on the words in poetical drama, above all where the words are remote from real life as well as in themselves exacting and difficult, the actors must move for the most part, slowly and quietly, and not very much, and there should be something in their movements decorative and rhythmical as if they were paintings on a frieze. They must not draw attention to themselves at wrong moments, for poetry and indeed all picturesque writing is perpetually making little pictures which draw the attention away for a second or two from the player. . . . Then, too, one must be content to have long quiet moments, long grey spaces, long level reaches, as it were — the leisure that is in all fine life: for what we may call the business-will in a hight state of activity is not everything, although contemporary drama knows of little else. (E176-77)

If the play is an image of the mind of its creator and if he sees beyond the hurry and press of this perishing world, the actors themselves in their total artistic context must avoid the 'old Ibsenite fury'[47] which possessed most of Yeats's contemporaries. If indeed the play is to convey 'love of the Unseen Life' (EI204), every single facet of its production must seek to project the timeless quiet of a 'wisdom no clock can measure' (B151).

It is now clear to most critics of the theatre, I think, that what may at first seem Yeats's more or less random comments about English drama and Irish disaffection becomes upon analysis a complete and consistent aesthetic of the theatre founded upon a Romantic faith in symbolic art. Against its fundamental cosmological and epistemological assumptions, Yeats measured his distaste for eighteenth-century abstraction, Victorian rhetoric, and contemporary realism. He experimented, he modified, he adjusted, and he developed; but he never lost faith. In 1898, he was convinced that 'The arts are . . . about to take upon their shoulders the burdens that have fallen from the shoulders of priests, and to lead us back upon our journey by filling our thoughts with the essences of things, and not with things. We are about to substitute once more the distillation of alchemy for the analyses of chemistry and for some other sciences; and certain of us are looking everywhere for the perfect alembic that no silver or golden drop may escape.'[48] The following year he admitted to the Editor of the *Daily Chronicle* that 'we will have difficulty at first, for some who do not dislike the modern theatre, or who dislike it for wrong reasons, will come to see our plays out of patriotism, and miss that appeal to the senses which they have mistaken for drama' (L311). By 1901 he had decided that 'It is possible . . . that we may have to deal with passing issues until we have re-created the imaginative tradition of Ireland, and filled the popular imagination again with saints and heroes' (E79). Thirty-five years later, at the end of his life, he was far less hopeful about the immediate future:

> I am convinced that in two or three generations it will become generally known that the mechanical theory has no reality, that the natural and supernatural are knit together, that to escape a dangerous fanaticism we must study a new science; at that moment Europeans may find something attractive in a Christ posed against a background not of Judaism but of Druidism, not shut off in dead history, but flowing, concrete, phenomenal. (EI518)

His scorn of a mechanistic theory of the universe and the arts and his conviction that 'the natural and supernatural are knit together' are still basic to his critical judgments and theories ('I was born into this faith, have lived in it, and shall die in it')[49]; but the millenium was far off, and the people who agreed with him were far fewer than he had anticipated in 1897 when he began seriously to organize a national 'theatre where the greatest passions and all the permanent interests of men might be displayed' (E313), to formulate the 'principles that may be applied to life itself' (EI219), and 'to search for the laws of what is perhaps a lost art' (L311).

38

'One has to go slowly,' Yeats wrote in 1906, 'perfecting first one thing and then another' (L477-78); six years later he was complaining to his father that 'it is always such a long research getting down to one's exact impression, one's exact ignorance and knowledge' (L568). It is worth observing, however, that in spite of some uncertainty and considerable modification, Yeats's theory and practice of the drama were consistently supported by sound aesthetic assumptions based upon old but always valid metaphysical doctrines. 'I cannot get it out of my mind,' he said in 1895, 'that this age of criticism is about to pass, and an age of imagination, of emotion, of moods, of revelation, about to come in its place; for certainly belief in a super-sensual world is at hand again' (EI197). This age, he hoped, would return 'poetical plays to the stage' (L327) which would emphasize the 'Other World' in the magic of the spoken word. 'This is really a magical revolution,' he wrote to George Russell, 'for the magical word is the chanted word' (L327). The drama, as Yeats observed to Robert Bridges, was obviously well suited for such a critical theory: 'I shall be altogether content if we can perfect this art for I have never felt that reading was better than an error, a part of the fall into the flesh, a mouthful of the apple' (L354). Yeats never wavered in his conviction 'that the poet seeks truth, not abstract truth, but a kind of vision of reality which satisfies the whole being.'[50] The artist cannot project his 'vision of reality' by copying the changing forms of this 'Vegetable Universe.' Yeats was certain that 'the end of art is the ecstasy awakened by the presence before an ever-changing mind of what is permanent in the world, or by the arousing of that mind itself into the very delicate and fastidious mood habitual with it when it is seeking those permanent and recurring things' (EI287). Synge, he observed bitterly a few days after his death, 'was but the more hated because he gave his country what it needed, an unmoved mind where there is a perpetual Last Day, a trumpeting, and coming up to judgment' (EI310). Yeats believed that the aim of criticism should be to prepare the imagination to accept an art which 'has made us look upon all with new eyesight' (EI287). In an essay about 'Moral and Immoral Plays,' he insisted that he had 'always been of Verhaeren's opinion that a masterpiece is a portion of the conscience of mankind' (E111). As a Platonist, Yeats was thereby reminding us than *con science* is the understanding born with us to apprehend the 'vision of reality.'[51] Although he concluded sadly in 1930 that 'all I wanted was impossible, and I wore out my youth in its pursuit,' he was firm in the conviction that his vision of truth would prevail: 'but now I know it is the mystery to come' (E313). As poet-prophet, he was supremely confident that he had made a lasting contribution to theatrical history: 'I have invented a form of drama, distinguished, indirect, and symbolic, and having no need of mob or Press to pay its way — an aristocratic form.'[52]

As a Romantic artist and critic, Yeats knew that all art is an 'imitation of something in the outer world,' and 'it often uses the outer world as a symbolism to express subjective moods.' That is, 'true art is expressive and symbolic, and makes every form, every sound, every colour, every gesture, a signature of some unanalysable imaginative essence.'[53] Although 'there will always be somewhere an intensity of pattern that we have never seen with our eyes' (L607), Yeats urges us to

> Hear the voice of the Bard!
> Who Present, Past, & Future, sees;
> Whose ears have heard
> The Holy Word
> That walk'd among the ancient trees. . . .(B210)

If at times Yeats seems less certain than his master Blake that the Holy Word could renew the fallen light, it was not because he was any less certain of the reality of the 'Unseen Life' or of the poet's mission to open the 'window into Eden.' For a significant part of his life the drama seemed to him the surest means of opening the clay-shuttered window, and he remained confident that 'a dramatic movement which will not die has been started' (E73). I am equally confident that the gradually evolving critical record of Yeats's 'ignorance and knowledge' of the theatre also represents an enduring monument. It most certainly is something more than 'thin dramatic theorizing.'

NOTES ON THE TEXT

1. The first important book to suggest the significance of Yeats's contribution to both theory and practice of the theatre is Una Ellis-Fermor, *The Irish Dramatic Movement* (London: Methuen, 1939). More recently, several full-length studies have been devoted to Yeats's plays: George Brandon Saul, *Prolegomena to the Study of Yeats's Plays* (New York: Octagon, 1971); Peter Ure, *Yeats the Playwright* (London: Routledge and Kegan Paul, 1963); Leonard E. Nathan, *The Tragic Drama of William Butler Yeats* (New York: Columbia University Press, 1965); John Rees Moore, *Masks of Love and Death: Yeats as Dramatist* (Ithaca: Cornell University Press, 1971). Other books consider selected plays: F. A. C. Wilson, *W. B. Yeats and Tradition* (London: Victor Gollancz, 1961); Helen Hennessy Vendler, *Yeats's Vision and the Later Plays* (Cambridge: Harvard University Press, 1963); S. B. Bushrui, *Yeats's Verse Plays: The Revisions 1900-1910* (Oxford: Clarendon Press, 1965); David R. Clark, *W. B. Yeats and the Theatre of Desolate Reality* (Dublin: The Dolmen Press, 1965). Also Edward Engelberg, *The Vast Design: Patterns in W. B. Yeats's Aesthetic* (Toronto: University of Toronto Press, 1964) devotes some attention to Yeats's dramatic theory. And many articles, too numerous to mention here, consider various details of his theory.
2. *The Drama of Chekhov, Synge, Yeats, and Pirandello* (London: Cassell, 1963), p. 344. Although Lucas does agree that 'some of his criticism was acute' (p. 277), he offers no examples, and his own criticism of Yeats's plays is so uniformly derogatory that one wonders why he devoted so much energy to a body of drama and theory he considered 'ghostly-thin.' 'As a producer,' Lucas concluded, 'Yeats appears to have been highly competent and observant, full of attention to dress and scenery, lighting and stage-business. But as a creator of serious drama, too introvert I think he remained; even though he toiled with tireless revision to make his plays more convincing' (p. 344).
3. *The Letters of W. B. Yeats*, edited by Allan Wade (New York: Macmillan, 1955), p. 595. To hold documentation to a minimum, I have adopted the following symbols for the standard Yeats editions frequently cited: L for *The Letters*, A for *Autobiographies*, E for *Explorations*, EI for *Essays and Introductions*. Hereafter, both symbols and page references are cited in the text.
4. See Ellis-Fermor, Chapter 4 ('Ideals in the Workshop') and Lady Augusta Gregory, *Our Irish Theatre* (New York: Capricorn Books, 1965), *passim*. A remark to Symons about the production of *The Shadowy Waters* will illustrate how conscious Yeats was of adjusting his plays to the demands of the stage and the audience: 'In one way finding it so bad has been a comfort, for it shows me how much I have learned by watching rehear-

sals in Dublin and by altering my plays and other people's for the stage' (L460).

5   *Blake : Complete Writings*, edited by Geoffrey Keynes (London : Oxford University Press, 1969), p. 629. Hereafter cited as B and followed by page numbers in the text.

6   *The Collected Works of William Butler Yeats* (Stratford-on-Avon : Shakespeare Head Press, 1908), IV, 87, 80. Yeats edited and wrote much of *Samhain*, 'an occasional review' which appeared irregularly from October 1901 to November 1908. It, like its predecessor *Beltaine* (1899-1900), served as 'the organ of the Irish Literary Theatre.'

7   See M. J. Sidnell, 'Hic and Ille : Shaw and Yeats,' *Theatre and Nationalism in Twentieth-Century Ireland*, edited by Robert O'Driscoll (Toronto : University of Toronto Press, 1971), pp. 156-78. As Sidnell points out (p. 159), Yeats admired Shaw's force : 'He could hit my enemies and the enemies of all I loved, as I could never hit, as no living author that was dear to me could ever hit' (A283). To Yeats, however, Shaw belonged to the old order : 'I saw Shaw today,' he wrote to Lady Gregory in a letter postmarked 12 March 1900; 'he came to the "Three Kings" on Saturday. I replied to a speech of his and pleased the Fellowship very much by proving that Shaw's point of view belonged to a bygone generation — to the scientific epoch — and was now 'reactionary.' He had never been called reactionary before. I think I beat him. He was not in very good form however' (L335; cited in Sidnell, p. 159). Sidnell 'suspects' that *John Bull's Other Island* 'was designed for performance in London and for rejection by the Irish National Theatre Company; and, moreover, that it was made with a lively interest in embarrassing and educating Yeats' (p. 166).

Although Shaw, Wilde, and George Moore 'seemed to have escaped from every National influence,' Yeats wrote in 1905, 'they never keep their heads for very long out of the flood of opinion,' and Shaw 'makes his comedies something less than life by never forgetting that he is a reformer' (E198). Synge, in contrast (and Yeats by implication), 'has no wish to change anything, to reform anything' (E1300).

But Yeats continued to admire Shaw, perhaps more than he was willing to admit. A letter to Florence Farr, a friend of both, is especially revealing : 'Did you see Bernard Shaw's letter in *The Times* a couple of days ago — logical, audacious and convincing, a really wonderful letter, at once violent and persuasive.' Yeats had seen *Caesar and Cleopatra* twice that week and was delighted with it despite its 'vulgarity' : 'Ah if he had but style, distinction, and was not such a barbarian of the barricades' (L500).

8   Quoted in *Our Irish Theatre*, p. 48.
9   *Ibid.*, p. 103.
10 *Ibid.*, pp. 48-49.

11 See Ellis-Fermor, pp. 47-48. She concludes: 'How much all that has followed in English drama from the beginning of the century to the present owes to their indefatigable courage and utter originality will never easily be estimated.'
12 Blake, p. 532. I have written an essay, not yet published, on the paradox of the creator as destroyer as it is treated in *Where There Is Nothing* and *The Unicorn from the Stars*.
13 E120. 'Thought takes the same form age after age,' Yeats wrote, 'and the things that people have said to me about this intellectual movement of ours have, I doubt not, been said in every country to every writer who was a disturber of the old life' (E121).
14 From *The Hour-Glass* (prose version), *The Variorum Edition of the Plays of W. B. Yeats*, edited by Russell K. Alspach (New York: Macmillan, 1966), p. 622.
15 This phrase is a kind of theme or thesis for *Where There Is Nothing* and its revision, *The Unicorn from the Stars*, though Martin Hearne is aware at the end of *The Unicorn* that he had deceived himself in believing that the destruction of the big house had served a valid social or religious function. It is useful, I think, to read these plays in conjunction with O'Casey's *Purple Dust*.
16 Allan Wade, *A Bibliography of the Writing of W. B. Yeats*, 3rd edition (London: Rupert Hart-Davis, 1968), p. 64. Published first in *The Bookman* (September, 1895), the essay was included in *Ideas of Good and Evil* (1903).
17 Blake, p. 150. This is one of the 'Proverbs of Hell,' a collection of revolutionary pronouncements which delighted Shaw as much as Yeats. See 'Maxims for Revolutionists,' published with *Man and Superman*.
18 Yeats is referring obliquely to his rejection of *The Silver Tassie* for the Abbey. He compared the early O'Casey to Synge and both of them to Joyce, who 'differs from Arnold Bennett and Galsworthy, let us say, because he can isolate the human mind and its vices as if in eternity' (E333).
19 L538. Yeats made this remark in a letter to Lady Gregory about a London production of *The Tinker's Wedding*: 'I have not had such a sensation of blind fury in a theatre for fifteen years.'
20 E333. The reference is to Blake, to whom this unholy trinity of false scientists symbolized the destruction of the imaginative life.
21 E102. 'In Ireland, wherever the enthusiasts are shaping life, the critic who does the will of the commercial theatre can but stand against his lonely pillar defending his articles of belief among a wild people. . . .' The implication is, of course, that the commercial critic's judgment is approved elsewhere. By the time of the *Playboy* controversy Yeats realized alas that most Irish critics were quite as bad as the English. See also E1283-84: 'Dramatic literature has for a long time been left to

criticism of journalists, and all these, the old stupid ones and the new clever ones, have tried to impress upon it their absorption in the life of the moment, their delight in obvious originality and in obvious logic, their shrinking from the ancient and the insoluble.' The point of the matter was Yeats's insistence that 'Drama is a means of expression, not a special subject-matter.'

22 *Beltaine* (April, 1900), III, 4. Yeats was writing about productions of *The Last Feast of the Fianna, Maive,* and *The Bending of the Bough.*
23 E417-18. These observations appeared in 'To-morrow's Revolution,' *On the Boiler,* p. 15 : 'We who are the opposites of our times should for the most part work at our art and for good manners' sake be silent.'
24 *Beltaine* (April, 1900), III, 4.
25 E165. Yeats refers to 'a certain guide-book to the stage published in France, and called *The Thirty-six Situations of Drama.*'
26 EI223. An observation in *Samhain* (1905) is especially interesting in this context : 'The scientific movement is ebbing a little everywhere, and here in Ireland it has never been in flood at all. And I am certain that everywhere literature will return once more to its old extravagant fantastical expression, for in literature, unlike science, there are no discoveries, and it is always the old that returns. Everything in Ireland urges us to this return, and it may be that we shall be the first to recover after the fifty years of mistake.

The antagonist of imaginative writing in Ireland is not a habit of scientific observation but our interest in matters of opinion' (E197). See my article on 'Yeats's Intellectual Nationalism,' *The Dublin Magazine,* IV (Summer, 1965), 8-26.

Compare also EI288 : 'The preoccupation of our art and literature with knowledge, with the surface of life, with the arbitrary, with mechanism, has arisen out of the root.'
27 EI171. Here, as he frequently did, Yeats contrasted the ancient world to the modern : 'But in Athens, where so many intellectual traditions were born, Euripides once changed hostility to enthusiasm by asking his playgoers whether it was his business to teach them, or their business to teach him.' In the same essay, 'The Theatre,' Yeats also contrasted the 'painted scenery' of the London stage with the poetic descriptions of the Greek.
28 *Beltaine* (February, 1900), II, 6.
29 E332-33. Compare E448 : 'The arts are all the bridal chambers of joy. No tragedy is legitimate unless it leads some great character to his final joy.' Yeats attributed this conception of tragedy to Lady Gregory : 'I have heard Lady Gregory say, rejecting some play in the modern manner sent to the Abbey Theatre, "Tragedy must be a joy to the man who dies" ' (EI523).
30 B471. Blake made this comment in direct opposition to a basic premise

of eighteenth-century epistemology, in particular that of John Locke. Blake reacted very strongly to the *Discourses* of Sir Joshua Reynolds primarily because 'Reynolds Thinks that Man Learns all that he knows' (B471). If Reynolds were right, Blake countered, all art would be 'Progressive,' and 'We should have had Mich. Angelos & Rafaels to Succeed & to Improve upon each other, But it is not so. Genius dies with its Possessor & comes not again till Another is Born with It' (B470). Since both Blake and Yeats insisted that they were secretaries to the real authors, who 'are in Eternity,' and that the function of art is 'to speak to future generations' (B825), they believed, in effect, that true art is recollection. Poet-prophets obviously would not concede that genius can be taught: 'Bacon's Philosophy has Destroy'd Art & Science' (B470).

31 S. L. MacGregor Mathers, trans., *The Kabbalah Unveiled* (London: Routledge and Kegan Paul, 1954), p. 155n. See also pp. 96n and 242-43n. Yeats knew this book well in its first edition, 1887. As one of the founding Chiefs of the Isis-Urania Temple of the Order of the Golden Dawn in London, Mathers himself was widely known to occultists in London and Paris. Yeats was initiated into the Order on 7 March 1890. See EI146.

32 L436. In a letter to Charles Ricketts on 26 July 1904 Yeats wrote: 'Those strange tales, with that curious wildness of theirs which is their compensation for lacking classic measure, and their sense of fine life, of a life that was lifted everywhere into beauty, are the energies, I think, behind all our movement here. I notice that when anybody here writes a play it always works out, whatever the ideas of the writer, into a cry for a more abundant and a more intense life.'

33 L475. Yeats was actually thinking more of the acting in such plays than of the plays themselves. Speaking of 'Mrs. Campbell and her generation,' he observed: 'This school reduces everything to an emotional least common denominator. It finds the scullion in the queen, because there are scullions in the audience but no queens. . . . A new school of acting is now growing up under the influence of the various attempts to create an intellectual drama, and of changes deeper than that. The new school seizes upon what is distinguished, solitary, proud even.' Yeats contrasted Mrs. Emery and Miss Darragh to Mrs. Campbell.

34 *Beltaine* (May, 1899), I, 6.

35 E167. Yeats may have been recalling a comment in A. P. Sinnett's *The Occult World*, a book he knew quite well: 'The truth which Madame Blavatsky would be the last person in the world to wish disguised, is that the assistance she derived from the Brothers, by occult agency, throughout the composition of her book, was so abundant and continuous that she is not so much the author of "Isis" as one of a group of *collaborateurs*, by whom it was actually produced' (London: Trubner, 1881, p. 159).

36 Quoted in *The Variorum Edition of the Poems of W. B. Yeats*, edited by Peter Allt and Russell K. Alspach (New York: Macmillan, 1957), p. 855.

37 El300. Yeats was writing about the people in Synge's plays. In the beginning, 'the players were puzzled by the rhythm' of his plays because 'no Irish countryman had ever that exact rhythm in his voice. . . . It makes the people of his imagination a little disembodied; it gives them a kind of innocence even in their anger and their cursing.'
38 See Kathleen Raine, *Yeats, the Tarot and the Golden Dawn* (Dublin: The Dolmen Press, 1972), pp. 28-30. Miss Raine suggests that Yeats helped 'Mathers in the writing of the Golden Dawn rituals' (p. 28).
39 *The Variorum Edition of the Poems*, p. 556. The line appears in 'Ribh Denounces Patrick.'
40 Among the many copies of rituals, flying rolls, lectures, etc. of the Yeats papers now in the possession of Senator Michael B. Yeats is a copy of the ritual for the Grade of Zelator ($1° = 10°$) with many revisions in Yeats's handwriting. He may have been referring to these revisions in a letter to Lady Gregory on 13 January 1902 : 'I have done a great deal of work at my Magical Rites, sketched them all out in their entirety' (L364). More likely, however, this reference is to a series of rituals he and Miss A. E. F. Horniman were preparing for his Celtic Mysteries. Modelled upon the rituals of the Golden Dawn, these also are incipient symbolic plays.
41 Raine, p. 30.
42 *The Variorum Edition of the Plays*, p. 970.
43 Yeats's comments on his own intentions in *The Countess Cathleen* may be applied to most of his plays :

> . . . he tried to suggest throughout the play that period, made out of many periods, in which the events in the folk-tales have happened. The play is not historic, but symbolic, and has as little to do with any definite place and time as an *auto* by Calderon. One should look for the Countess Cathleen and the peasants and the demons not in history, but . . . in one's own heart; and such costumes and scenery have been selected as will preserve the indefinite. *Beltaine* (May, 1899), I, 8.

44 Yeats's theory about the ideal union of scene and text was no doubt influenced by Blake's illuminated poems, especially the Prophetic Books, which are, like many of Yeats's plays, symbolic dramas of the soul's quest for paradise.
45 If we add to these lines just quoted the remainder of the paragraph, we have in effect a brief but convincing theory of the mask as well as Yeats's justification for going 'to Asia for a stage convention' :

> In poetical painting and in sculpture the face seems the nobler for lacking curiosity, alert attention, all that we sum up under the famous word of the realists, 'vitality.' It is even possible that being is only possessed completely by the dead, and that it is some knowledge of this that makes us gaze with so much emotion upon

the face of the Sphinx or of Buddha. Who can forget the face of Chaliapine as the Mogul King in *Prince Igor*, when a mask covering its upper portion made him seem like a phoenix at the end of its thousand wise years, awaiting in condescension the burning nest, and what did it not gain from that immobility in dignity and in power? (EI226-27)

46 See EI204 : 'But here in Ireland, when the arts have grown humble, they will find two passions ready to their hands, love of the Unseen Life and love of country.'

47 In a letter of 4 December 1902 Yeats wrote to Lady Gregory : 'Yes, I have written to Quinn, and I have had Joyce with me for a day. He was unexpectedly amiable and did not knock at the gate with his old Ibsenite fury' (L386). The early Joyce especially was most enthusiastic about Ibsen's work, as were Edward Martyn and George Moore among Yeats's colleagues in the Irish theatre.

48 EI193. At this stage of his career Yeats's critical theories were indebted to those of the French symbolists through Arthur Symons, but it should be noted that he is also using the conceptions and the language of the Golden Dawn : 'Mr. Symons understands these and other sentences to mean that poetry will henceforth be a poetry of essences, separated one from another in little and intense poems. I think there will be much poetry of this kind, because of an ever more arduous search for an almost disembodied ecstasy . . . (EI193-94). By the time this essay was reprinted in *Ideas of Good and Evil*, Yeats was readjusting his critical theories :

> The book is only one half of the orange for I only got a grip on the other half very lately. I am no longer in much sympathy with an essay like 'The Autumn of the Body,' not that I think that essay untrue. But I think I mistook for a permanent phase of the world what was only a preparation. The close of the last century was full of a strange desire to get out of form, to get to some kind of disembodied beauty, and now it seems to me the contrary impulse has come. (L402)

This letter to George Russell suggests in a reference to Apollonic and Dionysiac impulses that Nietzsche was at least partially responsible for the development of 'the contrary impulse' Yeats had developed by this time (14 May 1903). He was aware that *Ideas of Good and Evil* would have a special significance for occult readers : 'I would like to know what you think of the book, and if you could make your Hermetists read it I have a notion that it would do them a world of good' (L402). A letter to John Quinn on the day following expresses Yeats's reservations about a criticism 'too full of aspirations after remote things,' identifies Nietzsche as an agent of the change, and suggests the new direction his criticism will take : 'Whatever I do from this out will, I think, be more creative.

I will express myself, so far as I express myself in criticism at all, by that sort of thought that leads straight to action, straight to some sort of craft' (L403). It is clear from the context that the craft Yeats had in mind was that of the theatre.

49 EI518. This observation is part of the section on 'Subject-Matter' in 'A General Introduction for my Work' (1937).

50 L588. Yeats supported this observation by referring to 'Henry More, the seventeenth century platonist whom I have been reading all summer.'

51 Yeats's epistemological theories were perhaps influenced by Blake's sardonic observations, especially those in the marginalia on Reynolds's *Discourses*. Two will illustrate:

> I say These Principles could never be found out by the Study of Nature without Con — or Innate Science (B457).

> Knowledge of Ideal Beauty is Not to be Acquired. It is Born with us. Innate Ideas are in Every Man, Born with him; they are truly Himself. The Man who says that we have No Innate Ideas must be a Fool & a Knave, Having No Con-Science or Innate Science. (B459)

52 EI221. Yeats was writing in April 1916 about his experiments with the Noh plays. He acknowledged the 'help of Japanese plays "translated by Ernest Fenollosa and finished by Ezra Pound".'

53 EI140. 'False art,' he continued, 'is not expressive, but mimetic, not from experience but from observation, and is the mother of all evil. . . .' The allusion to Böehme's *Signature of All Things* reminds us again how much Yeats's critical theory, especially in the early essays, is indebted to the teachings of the Order of the Golden Dawn. As instructor of Mystical Philosophy in the Second Order, Yeats knew Böehme well.